Cat Dads

Your Guide to Feline Fatherhood

Cat Dads

Your Guide to Feline Fatherhood

Alison Davies

Illustrated by
Marie Åhfeldt

WHITE LION
PUBLISHING

Contents

'A kitten is in
the animal world
what a rosebud is
in the garden.'

ROBERT SOUTHEY

Introduction

There's something special about Cat Dads. I don't have to tell you that, because you either are one, know one or want to be one! We're led to believe that women have the monopoly on moggies, but that simply isn't true. Crazy cat lady may be the stereotype we're all used to, but there's nothing wrong with a little kitty worship, whoever you are. In truth, cats don't judge or prefer one sex to the other. They don't care who fills the food bowl or empties the litter tray, as long as it gets done (and to their exacting standard, I should add). The truth is, what you look like and your gender is less important than who you are inside. Cats go to the core. They have an uncanny ability of fixing you with a glaring stare that says, 'I see you, right to your roots!' There's no wriggling out of it, and you wouldn't want to, because Cat Dads know what a privilege it is to be appraised by your kitty; to look into those shining orbs and feel the love coming back at you in waves. Now, who wouldn't want that? Despite your protestations, cats have a way of wheedling themselves into your heart. Before you know it, you're

being crushed on the couch in a furry cat fuddle and loving every minute of it! As a Cat Dad you generally have certain attributes that set you apart from your female counterparts, from your laissez-faire approach to life with your feline to your love of collecting 'stuff' that your cat can stick its nose into.

Being a Cat Dad takes guts; you need confidence to deal with a creature of such discerning class. It takes dedication and skill – you may think a behind-the-ear rub is simply that, but you'd be wrong. It's about hitting the spot and going in for the scratch at exactly the right moment; should your timing be off, you might be on the receiving end of a sharp claw. It's about appreciating the gifts your cat gives you – which are manifold – and offering thanks by way of cheesy biscuits or deli smoked salmon, depending on your cat's predilection. It's about showing you care and being there in the wee small hours with the duvet and most of your bed, thinking outside the box, or with the box – in fact doing anything with the box except tossing it into the recycling!

Seasoned Cat Dads learn how to read the situation and know exactly what their cat wants by their expression and the way they hold themselves. They make it easier by presenting you with clues, and it's up to you to decipher them, a feat not beyond your daddy dexterities. Let's be honest, Cat Dads Do! They don't run for the hills at the sight of a leaping frog in their lounge or those curled shards of wallpaper that hang Freddy Kreuger-style from the hall. They go all out to make their cat the centre of their world, because Cat Dads are pawsome, and that's why this book is about you.

Within these pages you'll find a celebration of the men who love their cats. From tips and tools you need to keep handy, to a guide to decoding your kitty and a list of the benefits of being the best

Cat Dad in the world. You'll discover your puss parenting style and also how you can go the extra mile for your cat. If you want inspiration Insta-style, check out the social media Cat Dads who also make the grade. Whether you're a Cat Dad in the making, an old hand at feline fatherhood or a complete newbie, there's something here for you and, more importantly, for your cat.

On a serious note, this book is a thank you for all you do. For being loving and loved by your feline, for providing cuddles and laughter and patience by the bucket-load and for being there. Your cat thinks you're OK and that's all you really need to know, so sit back and enjoy this fête à feline. You are one top Cat Dad!

CHAPTER 1

Cat Dad Creed

'I simply can't resist a cat, particularly a purring one. They are the cleanest, cunningest, and most intelligent things I know, outside of the girl you love, of course.'

MARK TWAIN

How do you know if you're a Cat Dad? Well, that's easy – you just know. For starters, you live and breathe cat from the moment you are awoken by the dulcet tones of your feline's 'feed me' miaows to the end of day cuddles on the sofa. Your cat comes first, before beer, football and your significant other, before playing a round of golf or saddling up on your bike – unless you care to ride with your kitty by the side. And why not? You're a Cat Dad after all. That's what makes you special; you think outside the box and make your cat the centre of your world.

Not everyone makes the Cat Dad grade; it takes effort and a quirky sense of humour. Your cat will test your patience. From fussy eating to erratic moods, you'll experience the whole gamut of kitty craziness during your Cat Daddy journey, but that's what makes it so much fun. Just in case you're kitty clueless, the next page outlines the things that define you as a daddy of cats. Once you've ticked those off, you can go on to discover some of the other qualities that make you unique. Your cat knows it, the wider world knows it, and now you know it too.

You plan your cat's meals with care and flair, but just throw something together for yourself.

You've given them a cute nickname, or three!

You celebrate their birthday, and also buy them gifts at Christmas – any excuse to spoil them!

Birthday cards always come from you and the cat.

You're more than happy to let them steal most of the bed or your favourite spot on the sofa.

You have lengthy conversations with your cat, and truly believe they can understand you.

Your cat has more toys than Santa's workshop.

You're quite happy to shout their nickname at the top of your voice, even if the neighbours hear you calling for 'Miss Boo Boo Fluffy Bottom!'

You're a Cat Dad if...

You no longer care about the state of your home, furniture or clothes. Cat hair and scratches, what's not to love?

There are more pics of your cat on your phone than any other member of your family, including your other half!

You've set your cat up with its own Instagram account.

You don't care when they wake you at the crack of dawn for food – sleep is overrated!

You order things online just to get more cardboard boxes for your cat to explore.

You talk to your cat in a high-pitched baby voice that no one else (including your partner) will ever hear.

You talk about your cat constantly and find new ways to bring them into conversation.

Why Cat Dads are the Cat's Whiskers

Cat Dads rock and there are so many reasons why. It might not be obvious to you, but to your cat it's as clear as a fly on the windowsill. Of course they love you for you and all your human foibles, but there are other more 'manly' reasons why you're as good as catnip. To leave you in no doubt as to where you stand in the Cat to Human ratio, here are some of the key things that make you pawsome.

YOU'RE SCENT-SATIONAL

Let's get down to basics. Cats think humans stink, and it's true. To their delicate nostrils we pack a pungent punch. Which is no surprise when you consider that the average puss has 200 million sensors in their nose, as opposed to the average human who has a measly five million. No wonder your kitty can sniff that tuna before the can has been opened!

The smellier the human, the happier the cat. That's not to say that Cat Dads are a whiffy bunch – far from it. In fact, some Cat Dads are rather fragrant and take their beauty regime as seriously as a pampered Persian. The problem lies in the errant sock. You know the one – it made its break from the sweaty gym kit, missing the laundry basket entirely to land in a dishevelled heap on the bathroom floor, and it's **just** what your cat's been waiting for! From that first pounce they're in, covering themselves in every ounce of dad odour. While it might appear strange to you, it's actually their way of saying, 'You're in our club.' Cats like to mingle their scent with yours, to create a uniquely communal whiff, which lets the world know you're their Cat Father.

Missing Sock Syndrome could happen to anyone, but every cat worth its whiskers knows there's more chance of a hot-from-the-foot treat from their Cat Daddy. Just another reason why you're up there with catnip and cheesy biscuits!

PAWSOME TIP

A well-worn T-shirt is the purrfect comforter for a stressed-out cat in a carrier. You can easily calm their nerves on a trip to the vets with a top that smells of their Pop!

YOU FEIGN DISINTEREST

Ok, so we all know it's an act deep down, but cats can't resist it when you play hard to get. The more you ignore them, the more it intrigues them. Our felines are used to attention. Think of them as the animal kingdom's influencers; everywhere they go, a human will fall at their feet. Adoration is something they have come to expect. Thank the ancient Egyptians! They were so in love with all things feline, they practically worshipped the ground they pawed on, making them sacred in the eyes of the law. The result: your cat knows its place in the world.

As a bona fide Cat Dad, you recognize that it's not up to you to mollycoddle your moggie every time they walk in the room. You, like them, like a bit of freedom to do your thing, so instead of hanging off their every purr you pretend they're not there. And just like that, you're human catnip! Cats are curious by nature; if something enters their orbit, be it a fly, a sausage or a Cat Dad minding his own business, they need to check it out. Your relaxed body language is less threatening, putting puss instantly at ease, and allowing them space means they can greet you on their terms. A comfy lap and a few tummy tickles later and you're putty in their paws, but that was never in doubt, was it?

PAWSOME TIP

Need to get up close and personal with your cat? Maybe it's time for their regular flea and tick treatment? Instead of chasing them around the room, relax and let them come to you. Be patient and wait until they're snuggled close, then do your stuff. It will be less stressful for both of you!

YOU SHARE THE SAME SENSE OF HUMOUR

Goofy is your middle name, and while other humans might fail to be impressed by your dad jokes, your cat positively laps it up! Daftness is de rigueur, and the secret to your partnership. Let's be honest, felines are funny. Yes, they're majestic and graceful, clever and sleek, but they're also loopy as a lollipop. They appreciate your Cat Dad dance moves and the silly games you play to get their attention.

Your human partner in crime might look at you like you're a sandwich short of a picnic when you act like a clown, but your puss gets it. They understand the sudden urge to grasp a make-believe microphone and do a spot of high-pitched warbling, because they invented it – 3 a.m. caterwauling anyone?

Any moment is an opportunity to have fun, to run, to shake, to dribble and play the fool, all with your feline at your feet. As a Cat Dad, you're not afraid to let yourself go and seize the day with play, and that's the kind of cattitude that will take you far in the eyes of your puss. Others may call you eccentric, but do you really care when you've a feline friend to share the frivolity? You and your kitty are slapstick soul buddies, a real double act.

YOU APPRECIATE THEIR WILD SIDE

At heart, all felines are feral. They hunt, they fight, they stalk the night, they prowl and pounce without an ounce of remorse because that's who they are. And you wouldn't want it any other way because it's authenticity all the way with you. Cat Dads are Cat Dads. You're not ashamed of your true nature. You may try and hide it when you're out with the boys but put you in a room of cat ladies and you'll be in your element. Just like Clark Kent, the feline super dad will emerge!

You've learned to go with the flow, and if that means your cream leather sofa looks more like Shredded Wheat than designer chic, then so be it. Yes, there's a mouse family in residence in the upholstery thanks to a recent escapee of the long-tailed variety, but that's par for the course when you have a puss who likes to predate his playmates. You know this and accept it willingly because it's more important to have a happy cat and live in chaos than maintain a swish, super-polished flat.

And anyway, who are you to judge? You also like to walk on the wild side at times. Remember that week-old Chinese you found

lurking at the back of your fridge? From curled-up shrimps to crusty rice, most would have vetoed said offerings, but you like to live dangerously, and your cat approves. Together you are partners in crime, or is that grime? To be fair, Cat Dads are actually a clean and swanky bunch. You take the lead from your kitty, who also likes to keep on top of the personal grooming. Just because you're a tad devil-may-care, it doesn't mean you can't do it in style.

So, yes, you understand the wayward needs of your kitty and positively embrace them. You may worry when they go AWOL, but you're secretly in awe of their swagger and you wouldn't have it any other way. Your untamed tabby loves the freedom you give and returns the love with living, breathing gifts, and lots of rough and tumble, which is more than a fair trade as far as you're concerned. Then there are the sofa snuggles – not traditional Wild Cat/Big Boy behaviour, but I won't tell if you don't!

PAWSOME TIP

Impromptu play is a great way to train your cat. Rewards used in play, like toys and treats, can be used to promote good behaviour at other times. For example, if your cat learns that every time they respond to their name during a game, they get a treat, they'll learn to respond to it at other times too.

YOU ARE PATIENT

One universal trait all Cat Dads encompass is empathy. It's the ultimate superpower when it comes to all thing's kitty, and it's what makes you the most patient of parents. You might assume all feline lovers share this tolerance, but Cat Dads take it to the next level. Your deep human-to-kitty connection goes without saying, but your unflappable nature comes from a fascination with all things feline and a need to do things right.

Your cat astounds you every day. They're an enigma clothed in fur, and that's what makes them so irresistible and all round entertaining. Everything about them piques your interest – the good, the bad and the feline-feeling ugly, because it all comes from the same stirringly purring place.

Yes, they make you scratch your head sometimes and when they refuse their food for the third time after opening a fresh and flavoursome pouch it might drive you nuts, but it's their prerogative as a puss to make a fuss. They are not here to be fully understood, they are here to be worshipped – something Cat Dads do exceedingly well. Most chaps aren't overtly romantic when it comes to affairs of the heart, but feline loving is a different kettle of fish. Just one look at those baby blues and you're a smitten kitten and willing to go the extra mile with a smile. Some might call it 'long-suffering', but they would be wrong. Scratches and clawing aside, there is no pain, only long-term gain in loving a cat, and Cat Dads do it freely, happily and with a passion – something any kitty worth its whiskers would concede.

PAWSOME TIP

Your cat needs to scratch. It's instinctive and it's good for them, as it helps to remove dead nails and keep their claws in tip-top condition. Make sure you have plenty of scratching posts and boards around the house to give your furniture and walls a break!

'What greater gift than the love of a cat?'

CHARLES DICKENS

CHAPTER 2

What Type of Cat Dad Are You?

'Time spent
with cats is
never wasted.'

SIGMUND FREUD

Cat Dads come in all shapes and sizes. Whether you're a natural puss parent or you've had to work at it, at the end of the day you'll want the same things – a happy cat and a nice life together. There will be moments when your cat's a conundrum and others when you just can't get enough of your ball of fluff; it doesn't matter how much you prepare for it, sharing your world with a cat is as unpredictable as it is joyous.

How you approach the role of Cat Dad is entirely up to you and the kind of person you are. Maybe you're a doting daddy who likes to put them on a pedestal, or you consider yourself your feline's BFF. Perhaps you're a prankster dad who loves to play silly with your kitty, or the love/ hate kind – aloof on the surface but cat-crazy when it counts! Maybe it's not how you are but what you know that makes the difference and helps your feline to feel loved. Whichever way you roll, whether you're hands on or hands off, this quiz reveals your puss parenting style, along with tips on how to strengthen your special bond and take it to the next level. Happy puss parenting!

QUIZ

1) You're off to work for the day, but before you go you always...
a) Fill the food bowls and give your kitty a cuddle
b) Say 'goodbye' to your puss
c) Check the cat flap is open
d) Have a quick game of 'chase the feather' with your feline
e) Fill the automated feeder ready for your cat's timed lunch

2) While you're at work, you spend your time...
a) Boring your colleagues with cute pics of your cat
b) Wondering what your furry friend is up to and wishing you were there
c) Thinking about what you can have for tea that won't be of interest to your cat
d) Devising fun tricks you can play on your feline
e) Perusing your state-of-the-art camera system, to check what your cat is up to

3) In the evening you like to...
a) Snuggle up with your cat on the sofa
b) Talk to your kitty – you're sure they understand what you're saying
c) Get on with whatever needs doing, and if your cat wants to join in, that's fine
d) Play a game of 'hide the sock' with your puss
e) Watch your cat chase the pretty lights from your laser pointer

4) When feeding your cat you always...

a) Go for gourmet dishes – only the very best for your kitty

b) Go for what they like – it might not be the most expensive, but they wolf it down

c) Go for what's on offer – if they're not fussed, a few titbits from your dinner will keep them happy

d) Like to surprise them with interesting food choices and brand new flavours

e) Weigh everything to ensure they're getting the right amount to keep them in shape

5) What's your favourite thing to do with your cat?

a) Anything you do with your cat is awesome, you just love spending time with them

b) Hanging out together, chilling in front of the TV or in the garden

c) I don't have to 'do' anything, my cat follows me around

d) Playing games keeps us both happy and fit

e) Insta posts, Facebook, TikTok, we're into our social media

6) Spending time with your feline makes you feel...

a) Loved and needed

b) Happy and relaxed

c) Amused and bemused

d) Energized and upbeat

e) Responsible and caring

7) What's your grooming routine like?

a) Once a day the brush comes out for their coat, and sometimes the shampoo too

b) It's not so much grooming as a thorough stroke and fur ruffle whenever they need it

c) They don't need your help with that

d) I try to make it a game, and use the comb like a toy when I can get hold of them

e) I use my eco-friendly de-shedding glove once a week

8) Your cat's gone AWOL. What do you do?

a) Panic! You pace the streets for hours calling their name
b) Put out some of their favourite foodie treats to tempt them back home
c) I'm not worried, they'll come home when they're ready
d) Appeal to their sense of fun by shaking their smelliest, loudest toy while walking the length of the garden
e) I know where they are, there's a cat cam attached to their collar

9) It's the dreaded visit to the vets. How do you keep your cat calm?

a) Lots of stroking and cuddles does the trick
b) Soothing words seem to calm my kitty
c) I try to minimize fuss and focus on getting in and out of the vet quickly
d) I put a catnip mouse in the carrier
e) I spray a comforting herbal scent on their travel blanket

10) What's the best thing about being a Cat Dad?

a) Everything! My cat is my world
b) Building the trust between you
c) There's always something to laugh about
d) Each day is a new adventure
e) Learning what makes my cat tick

The Results

IF YOU'RE MOSTLY A'S, YOU'RE A DOTING DADDY

Nothing is more important than your kitty. It's not that you're obsessed or anything... Well ok, maybe a little! You live and breathe cat from the moment you wake up in the morning at stupid-o-clock to make sure your feline is fed and watered, to the second your head hits the pillow (that is, if there's space because it's your cat's favourite place to snooze). And why wouldn't you be? Just look at them! Talk about fur finesse, it's no wonder they deserve the best, and that's what you give them. From the softest, squishiest cat igloos to top-of-the-range foodie delicacies to tantalize their taste buds, nothing is too much trouble for your fur bubba. And that's the point, they're your baby first and foremost. You exist to serve their needs and they exist to be adored; it's a match made in heaven. Of course not everyone feels the same way, and you're sure to experience clueless stares and eye-rolling from your cat-less mates when you bring out your phone for the thousandth round of picture sharing, but who cares?

PAWSOME TIP

Allow your bond to breathe by giving your kitty space and reducing the treats. Make them work for it by using a treat ball to dispense the goodies. This will encourage them to move and play, which is more fun for them and gives you time to enjoy your kitty from afar.

IF YOU'RE MOSTLY B'S, YOU'RE A FELINE BESTIE

Cloud nine is where it's at when you're chilling with your cat. The quiet understanding you share is fur-to-skin deep, and at times it seems like you don't need words at all – not that it stops you! There's nothing you like more than coming through the door and sharing the goss with your gorgeous puss. From wet-nosed kisses to playful hisses, it's all par for the course on the road to feline fatherhood. You're convinced your cat can read your mind but that's because they've come to know your ways, just as you've taken the time to get to know their furry foibles. Understanding is a two-way street, and you'll cross it together, paw in hand. Patience is the key to your special relationship, and while you never know what's around the corner, be it a coughed-up furball or pouncing puss, you're ready for the challenge. Your cat is your happy place, and the feeling is mutual. You're two peas in a fuzzy pod, but what's a little cat hair between friends!

IF YOU'RE MOSTLY C'S, YOU'RE A COOL COMPANION

Cool as a cucumber on the surface, you're the kind of Cat Dad who likes to keep things under wraps. Even so, you've still quite a passion for your puss – you just keep it on the down-low. You're probably quite a stylish dude with a laid-back attitude. Taking it slow is the way to go, and that's how it is in all things. You'll never corner your cat for a cuddle; you prefer the softly, softly approach, taking time and treats to the next level. OK, so we know you hide them about your person, then pretend to not be bothered. Either that or your aftershave is eau de catnip. Whichever way you do it, your cat is a heat-seeking missile and you are the prize. They can't get enough of your laissez-faire charm, clinging to your arm, leg or any other body part within grasping distance, and in return you appreciate their kookiness. You're an unconventional twosome, but there's never a dull moment when you're in the same room, and that, my friend, is enough to make anyone's heart go 'boom!'

PAWSOME TIP

Build the rapport by having some fun together with a game of hide and seek. They'll love the attention, and you'll secretly enjoy the thrill of the chase!

IF YOU'RE MOSTLY D'S, YOU'RE A PRANKSTER DAD

It's joy all the way with you two. Spending time with your cat brings out your inner child, and your puss adores being in your orbit because you keep them entertained. From an impromptu game of 'seek the slipper' to an all-out frenzy the length and breadth of the living room, it's all to play for. You look forward to those end of the day gaming sessions and you're always one step ahead when it comes to the fun factor. Your cat approves of your on-the-ball style and the fact that you go the extra mile to break the boredom. You're probably quite sporty yourself and like to keep active, which means you'll always have the time and energy to devote to your puss, but pleasure isn't the only form of leisure they appreciate. Quiet time spent cosying up can also strengthen the bond between you, while giving you a moment or two to recharge ready for the next battle!

IF YOU'RE MOSTLY E'S, YOU'RE A HIGH-TECH POP

It's go-gadget-go in your state-of-the-art abode. If it isn't automated, it soon will be. You're all about saving time and making things super-efficient for both of you. It's not that you want to cut corners or avoid one-on-one time with your puss – for you it's all about living your best life together in high-tech harmony. Everything goes and flows, with sleek and minimal chic to make your life run smoothly, but that doesn't mean you aren't up for a bit of spontaneous silliness should the need arise. You just want your cat to have everything it needs to survive and thrive in the busy and sometimes confusing world of social media, and that includes a presence. OK, so they might not understand the nuances of moggie memes or how many TikTok followers they have, but you like to think they're popular, because to you they're the cat's whiskers. Learning about your cat is what really makes you tick, and you won't stop until you're well versed in all things feline. Just remember, clever gizmos aside, they think you're pretty pawsome too!

'I believe cats to be spirits come to earth. A cat, I am sure, could walk on a cloud without coming through.'

JULES VERNE

CHAPTER 3

Cat Dad Toolkit

'A kitten is
the delight of
a household.
All day long a
comedy is played
out by an
incomparable
actor.'

CHAMPFLEURY

Cat Dads play an important role in their cat's life. It's more than just being there; it's about showing you care in as many different ways as you can. Your cat's needs are numerous, as you will already have discovered. It's up to you as chief sachet opener to respond and serve, and do it with style and a smile!

To assist you on your quest, here's a list of some of the best Cat Dad tools, the ones that will really make life easier and fun for both of you – yes, these are things you should appreciate too! The items on this list will help you understand what your cat really needs, and how you can help them live their best life. They're practical, easily sourced and they might even inspire you to come up with other additions to the moggie/daddy toolkit.

There's also a checklist at the end of this chapter with useful suggestions for items that will help with your cat's general health and wellbeing. It's all about keeping them in the manner they're accustomed to – in other words, tip-top condition and ready to prowl the catwalk!

The Toolkit

THE CARDBOARD BOX

The cardboard box is the toy of choice for the curious cat. It is everything and nothing, and it will drive them nuts. Part of the beauty of this toolkit essential is that you benefit too! As a collector of 'stuff', you're the perfect partner for a puss. Think of all the delightful high-tech and absolutely useless items you can order online. It matters not if the item is as practical as a chocolate teapot, you're not really doing it for you; your actions are selfless and motivated by your moggie's need for cardboard.

In its purest state, the box, whatever the shape, is a place of sanctuary and the ideal spot to hide, stalk prey and remain safe from roaming predators, including the vacuum cleaner. Not only that, but it's also super-toasty to curl up in. What's not to love?

PAWSOME TIP

Boost your cat's fitness by creating a cardboard-box assault course. You can spend hours faffing around cutting random holes in the boxes or sticking two or three together to create a tunnel that your kitty can explore.

THE SPORTS BAG

A must for Cat Dads and kitties alike. Whether you're a football afficionado, a gym-goer or a tennis buff, you'll need a bag to store and transport your kit. More importantly, it's a great place to hide sweaty items and other miscellaneous stuff – think energy bars and sweet treats for that pre-match boost! But it's just as important to your cat. There's an unwritten rule that felines must vet any bag with which they come into contact. After all, anything with an opening the size of a cat's head is fair game to explore.

The beauty of the sports bag is the fabric! Stretchy, smelly, masculine layers filled with all your stuff – it's cat Heaven with a capital H. The depth, strength and flexibility make it the purrfect place for a good wriggle, and the sausage-like shape provides ample space to flex those paws while being cocooned in softness. Not to mention the fact that it smells of you!

Of course, we'll never know how the feline fascination with bags first began, but it's as deep-rooted as those scratch marks on your sofa, so you might as well succumb. Invest in the bag – you know you want to! It will provide hours of fun for both of you.

THE TOOL BOX

Whether you fancy yourself as a handyman or you're clueless when it comes to wielding a hammer, you're sure to have noticed your cat's fascination with all things DIY. You only have to reach for a spanner to get your kitty excited. It's more than just the tools, of course. While a screwdriver has its merits, your moggie is more interested in what you do with it and will at every opportunity offer you advice in the form of an encouraging miaow. It doesn't matter if your tools are shiny and new or from the Ark, their appeal is manifold from the way they look to the musty scent and the cloppetty-clanky sounds they make, even if you don't know what you're doing with them. The fact that you play with them means they must be good. It's no wonder your kitty is hooked.

Of course, tools can be dangerous in the wrong paws, so to avoid any DIY disasters invest in some interestingly shaped, bright and noisy toys for your cat. Just like us, cats crave stimulation and they like new things that they haven't seen before, so while you don your hard hat, set your puss to work with its own soft toy toolkit. That way you'll both have fun.

Cat Dad Warning: do not attempt to put up wallpaper in the company of your cat. It will end badly... think Kitty Claw Massacre!

THE TREAT CUPBOARD

This is another essential, and the good news is you've probably got one of these already. Don't be coy, every boy has a snack cupboard, even if they haven't given it an official title. Yours is probably stuffed with your favourite salty snacks and biscuits. Your partner/roommate/friends know it too, and your cat most definitely knows it! With a nose stuffed with scent sensors, there's no fooling the feline, so don't even try.

If you want to keep your treat cupboard intact, you can go one of three ways. First, you can throw caution to the wind and let them fill their furry boots, making sure all snacks are feline-friendly. Second, you can give them their own treat cupboard. Or, third, you can lock that sucker up like Fort Knox. **Note: child locks might work for a time, but your cat is clever and will see this as laying down the snack gauntlet. Be warned!**

The second option is probably your best move, and this is what makes it an essential on the toolkit. You'll hopefully keep your snacks safe while allowing your kitty free run of their own tabby tuck shop. It's a statement that says, 'You're just like one of the lads, so here's a little corner of food heaven for you!' Or, if you want to be blunt, 'Keep your paws off my patch!'

THE LOFTY BOLT-HOLE

This is exactly what it says on the tin. It's a safe stroke-free space that human hands can't reach. It's not so much a tool as a necessity, which gives your kitty security in a moment of crisis – like when the doorbell rings and a well-meaning neighbour pops in for a chat, or the plumber arrives to service the boiler. It even works as a 'friend or foe' decider, giving your cat breathing space to work out if your Great Aunt Hetty is a secret cat catcher or just a sweet old lady who loves all things feline. It's the kitty equivalent of a man shed, which makes it something you not only understand but appreciate.

As a Cat Dad, it's your job to protect and respect your kitty, to allow for those moments when they want to be alone. By giving them a hideout with a view, it's your way of saying, 'You do you.' The Cat Daddy knows a bit of freedom goes a long way to boosting the feline feel-good vibes.

To help your cat feel even more secure, position their favourite cushion/blanket in said space – and, yes, that means on top of the refrigerator, the wardrobe or wherever their bolt-hole may be. Make it a cat-friendly zone with a few home comforts and you'll be top Cat Dad, for at least a minute or two!

KEYS

There's something mystical about keys. Maybe it's the fact that keys unlock doors that might otherwise remain shut to your kitty, or perhaps it's something more superficial, like the noise they make and the way they glint in the sunlight. One thing is certain, keys are captivating if you're a cat, which makes them a must-have for the Cat Dad toolkit.

Whether your preference is a super-swish car, camper van, motorbike or bicycle, you're going to need keys. From keys to get in and start it, to keys that lock it up, keys to the garage, keys to the shed where you store your bits, you've always got a bunch to hand. This also means you've got a toy on tap for those off-the-cuff moments when you need to distract your cat, simply whip out your keys and give them a jingle; you'll instantly have their full attention.

CRAZY CAT DAD MUG

This is one for you. Any Cat Dad worth his fur-covered T-shirt must have a Crazy Cat Dad Mug. Consider it a badge of honour, a way to wear your kitty stripes loud and proud. Yes it's twee and a cliché, but who cares? You're a Cat Dad after all. You're not bothered about such things.

If you've learned anything from watching your feline, it's the importance of being true to yourself and accepting yourself for who you are. When you're a cat person you understand that life is for living, that every day is an opportunity to have fun, to chase the butterfly or laze in the sun, or simply have a good scratch because you can. Your cat has taught you this, and now you must live it. Seize the moment and seize the mug. You know you want to. Your feline demands it!

'When a man loves cats, I am his friend and comrade, without further introduction.'

MARK TWAIN

Cat Dad Cupboard Essentials

COTTON WOOL PADS

Great for bathing small cuts and cleaning eyes and ears.

GROOMING BRUSH

A regular grooming routine will help with furballs.

PILL DISPENSER

At some point you will need to give your cat a pill, and a dispenser makes the process slightly easier. Worth a try if you value your fingers.

HIBISCRUB

Good for treating skin problems and general hygiene.

SUN CREAM

Your cat can get sunburned too! Rub a tiny amount into the ears and on the nose.

VASELINE

Cats can get constipated, and a dab of Vaseline on the bottom will make going to the loo easier. It also acts as a barrier to frost and ice on paws on winter days.

TWEEZERS

For hard-to-remove items lodged in fur or paws.

CARPET CLEANER

Vomit, poop or a gooey furball – it's inevitable that you will face one or all of these things. Be prepared and invest in a good pet carpet cleaner.

CHAPTER 4

Decode Your Cat

'The smallest feline is a masterpiece.'

LEONARDO DA VINCI

When you become a Cat Dad, there's no fanfare, certificate or lap of honour, and there's certainly no manual that tells you how to communicate with your furry friend. Cats are not like cars; you can't flip the bonnet and have a poke around or take them out for a test drive. You're thrown in at the deep end and, together with a little patience, you learn how to read your cat and discover what makes them tick. Every puss is different, and will have quirks, feline foibles and a personality that's distinctly theirs, but there are certain things cats do that are universal.

The basics of kitty communication are easy, it's all about the non-verbal – those nuances of movement and body language that reveal your cat's true feelings. Ok, so men don't have the best track record at picking up subtle signals, particularly when it comes to women, but cats are different. Simple things like the way they hold themselves and how they use different parts of the body can illustrate exactly how your feline feels, as well as what they think of you. You can decode your cat, and even have a conversation, just by giving them the once over and taking note of the little things. It's time to get up close and furry with your feline and strengthen that daddy-to-kitty bond, with a checklist on what to look out for.

THE TAIL

If in doubt, look at the tail. It's the kitty version of a thermometer and gives you a reading of your moggie's mood. Learning what the different positions mean will help you understand how your feline is feeling at any given moment. It's your first port of call when it comes to communication with your cat.

Tail Raised

Nothing says, 'Hey, I'm here. It's me!' more than a tail at full mast. It's like a flag, heralding the presence of your most precious puss, and signals that all is well in their world and they're feeling chilled. Should the tip be hooked, then you're in the company of a confident and happy cat. Well done you.

Tail-Tip Wiggle

This is the pinnacle of puss pleasure. The tail-tip wiggle looks like the tiniest tremor and is a clear sign your kitty is on cloud nine. Usually reserved for those ten-out-of-ten tuna moments, when nothing else (except maybe a slice of smoked salmon) will do. It's the feline version of a dancefloor shimmy, and is often coupled with a deep belly purr. This move, when it occurs in quick succession during stroking, means you've made it. You are the Cat Dad of Cat Dads, and you know what makes your feline feel divine!

Tail Wagging

While it's a clear sign of joy in dogs, for cats the tail wag is a big red flag. It means 'Don't come near, I'll spear you with a razor sharp claw'. An instant sign of displeasure, when it first begins it is gentler and an indication that your cat feels agitated and wants some space. If you're foolish enough to stick around during those early stages, you'll see the wagging pick up speed, until what started as a flap becomes a frantic slap. By then it's too late; you should have run for cover ages ago. You'll likely be confronted with a warning growl. Should the tail inflate 1960s bouffant style, then stand back, your cat is ready to attack and fur is about to fly!

Tail Down

This is a frown, feline style, a sign that your cat is feeling vulnerable and defensive. An 'aggressive' frown might be coupled with a hiss and ears right back, while an 'under the weather' frown might make your moggie hunch down and wrap its tail around its body. You know your cat better than anyone else, so play it by ear. It could be that your cat's just in a grump – a run-in with a territorial tabby could be enough to put your cat in a huff. Trust your Cat Dad instincts, and if in doubt seek out a professional.

PAWSOME TIP

Lots of cats suffer with discharge, which collects in the corner of their eye. To help, bathe their eyes regularly with warm water and cotton wool pads to remove any dried-on dirt and prevent infections.

THE EYES

The eyes have it, or so they say, and it's never more true than when it comes to your cat. According to the ancients, your cat's eyes were not only the window to their soul, but also a portal to the fairy otherworld. Should you dare to stare, you might catch a glimpse of the fairy king and queen peeking back at you. It may be a little farfetched, but there's some truth to the idea. The inky depths of your puss's peepers present a deeper picture of their emotions, so if you want to see the look of love, look no further.

The Long, Slow Blink

You're a wonderful Cat Daddy indeed if you witness one of these! It's that 'I love you' moment, with shiny bells on it. It starts with a soft and appraising stare, and then the blink begins. This is not a quick affair. It might look like your cat is about to nod off, but don't be fooled, your feline is feeling the love and then some. Enjoy, engage and endeavour to return the favour with a long, slow blink of your own. Yes, it may feel strange, but your cat will instinctively respond, and you'll strengthen the bond between you. Feline Love Fest anyone?

The Stare

The stare comes in many forms. A relaxed gaze says, 'I'm here, you're there, and I'm interested in you and what you do.' It's a clear sign that your cat is trying to connect. The fervour behind the stare is where it's at. Depending on the intensity, it can go from 'I'm keeping an eye on you,' to a territorial 'You lookin' at me, punk?'

The general rule when confronted with a stare of the steely variety is to look away. Do not let yourself be drawn in, because the simple fact is that you will never win. Your cat has learned from day one that staring is an art form and a way of tracking prey, so unless you want to end up in the feline equivalent of a bar brawl, retreat, retreat, retreat!

THE BODY

Posture is everything to the discerning puss. How they hold their body and what they do with it will tell you all you need to know about their mood and how they relate to you.

Bottom Butt

You know this move. You've settled down in front of your favourite TV programme with a cat on your lap. All is rosy cosy, then for some bizarre reason your cat does a 180 and sticks its butt slap bang in your face. Charming! It's enough to put you off your salted peanuts – well, almost. The fact is that this little about-turn is an act of love. Yes, really! It is a sign of companionship and trust; by revealing their most vulnerable parts, your pet is saying, 'I believe you won't hurt me because you love me'.

Your cat sees and experiences the world through scent, and this includes how they interact with you. It's all about the anal glands. The slightest pong provides enough info for your puss to read another kitty and tell how they feel, where they've been and what makes them tick. When they let you have a good sniff of the whiff, they're saying, 'This is me.' So, rather than being offended when your cat does a butt-face manoeuvre, be happy. You're their Cat Dad and they love, love, love you!

Head Butt

A head butt is a feline high five. It's a 'Hey, you're cool' manoeuvre reserved for the best of Cat Dads. Dispensed in one swift but gentle nudge, it can be delivered to the ankles, legs, arms, face or any other exposed body part. It's not aggressive, it's actually a sign of adoration, usually followed by a lingering body brush. What more could you ask for? Except maybe a lint roller!

Zoomies

So called because that's the sound your cat would make if it had an engine. When your cat goes from snooze to rapid cruise in a second, and suddenly that calm Sunday afternoon nap becomes a free-for-all as your feline speeds from room to room, taking half the furniture with it, then my friend you've been 'zoomed'.

It looks like they're in hot pursuit of prey, or maybe being chased by an invisible foe. Either way, it's a frantic sight, but never fear, this is perfectly natural and comes from a need for action. Your cat just wants to have fun! They could have been away with the fairies moments before, but suddenly they're awake and looking for trouble. You're welcome to join in the fun, or simply sit back and watch the show.

THE EARS

Your cat's ears are like mini antennae, ready to absorb the slightest nuance of sound. From the gentle shuffle of a tiny beetle in the undergrowth to the monstrous roar of your vacuum cleaner, your tabby's tabs do not miss a trick! After all, how would your cat hear the delicate ding of the tin opener if it wasn't for this super sense? The ears also illustrate a range of emotions; whether it's that first prickle of fear or the tentative tingle of excitement in the air, it's there, in the ear.

Ears Back

This denotes a stressed-out kitty, and if they're pressed back, then an attack could be in the offing. Irritation is at the heart of this move, and your puss is feeling the pressure. Whether they're scared, annoyed or just over-stimulated, it's a good idea to leave well alone. Look to the body for other clues and go with your gut. If they're hunched into a ball, they're trying to make themselves look small because they feel exposed. A fluffed up, thrashing tail is a definite 'claws out' move. Step away from the kitty right now!

Ears Straight Up

When your cat's ears are straight up, they're in normal mode. Their environment is calm and they feel at ease. From this position it could go either way, depending on outside stimulus.

Ears Forward

Similar to straight up, this cat is feline fine with a capital F for Fab-mew-less. They're on top of their game, alert and in a playful mood. If the ears are twitching, it's likely something has piqued their interest, so prepare for your puss to pounce, flounce or announce their presence, while seeking adventure or something else to occupy their time. As long as they're having fun, that's all that really counts.

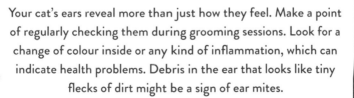

PAWSOME TIP

Your cat's ears reveal more than just how they feel. Make a point of regularly checking them during grooming sessions. Look for a change of colour inside or any kind of inflammation, which can indicate health problems. Debris in the ear that looks like tiny flecks of dirt might be a sign of ear mites.

Cat Body Language and What it Really Means

Ever wondered what your cat would say if it could talk to you? Ponder no more. Check out these common Cat Dad scenarios and discover what your cat is really thinking...

SCENARIO #1 – VINYL VICTIM

It's been a long day and you fancy spinning the decks and giving some of your old albums a play, but your cat is splayed, legs akimbo on the record player, giving its bottom some serious attention.

What this means in Cat Speak: 'If you think you're going to insult my tender eardrums with that racket, you're one deluded daddy. Pay me, your sweet fur baby, some attention and I might let you stick on something appropriate. 'Year of the Cat' anyone?'

In other words... your cat is bored and looking for something to do. A quick game of chase the catnip mouse would perk them up and also free up your turntable.

SCENARIO #2 – BED BUG

From rolling, spreading, scrunching up the bedding, burping, shaking and still not waking, you've got the moves when it comes to bedtime, but there's one problem. You're just about to stretch out and strut your stuff, when your cat does a dive bomb on to your chest and pins you in place with its paws.

What this means in Cat Speak: 'Sleepy daddy, you are by far my mattress of choice! There is no escape from my clutches, so please do not try. We are in this together. Repeat after me, one Cat Dad, two Cat Dad... zzz.'

In other words... your cat is looking for reassurance (or body heat). A snuggle will soothe you both to sleep.

SCENARIO #3 – STIR-FRY

It's quick, it's easy, it uses up all the curled-up veg at the back of your fridge – what's not to love about a cheeky mid-week stir-fry? It's the food of Gods and Men, and you're a dab hand at it too. You've got the sizzle going and you're doing your best Gordon Ramsay impression when your cat winds its body and tail around your ankles, fixing you to the spot.

What this means in Cat Speak: 'Daddy dearest, what delights are you cooking up just for me? Can I smell prawns, or perhaps chicken? I am practically wasting away here, see how thin, and lithe my body has become as I wrap myself around you! Feed me! Feed me! FEED ME!'

In other words... your cat is hungry. If they've just eaten or it isn't their usual mealtime, a quick cat treat or a biscuit will keep them from snaffling your supper.

SCENARIO #4 – MIRROR MIRROR

From a quick primp and polish to full-on male preening, time spent in front of the bathroom mirror is key for any man about town, never mind a Cat Dad with places to be! Whether you're mid-pluck of ear fluff or slapping on the moisturizer, you find you have a furry audience at your feet, giving you a swift nip to the shins in the process.

What this means in Cat Speak: 'Hey Daddio! Watcha doing? Call that grooming? You and I both know you will never be as beautiful as I am, so you might as well call it day, get down here and give me some sugar. You know you want to!'

In other words... your cat is seeking attention. Share the love and give them a five-minute grooming session to untangle their fur and maintain a sleek and shiny coat.

'When I play with my cat, who knows if I am not a pastime to her more than she is to me?'

MICHEL DE MONTAIGNE

CHAPTER 5

The Benefits of Feline Fatherhood

'I have studied many philosophers and many cats. The wisdom of cats is infinitely superior.'

HIPPOLYTE TAINE

As a Cat Dad you'll know what an **honour it is to share your life with a feline.** From their sock-stealing antics to cosying up together in the evening or muscling in on screentime during your work Zoom meeting, you are truly blessed, and your cat thinks so too! Let's not forget, they were once revered around the world and treated like gods. Even in the darkest of days during the Middle Ages in Britain, some believed they were witches with the power to transform and cast spells – look how well they've got you dancing to their tune!

There's something supremely magical about cats, from their lithe and graceful walk to the mystical glint in their eyes. But even if you don't believe in all that hocus-pocus, a no-nonsense fella will understand the special nature of all things feline. Just by being present in your life, they're bestowing an abundance of gifts in your lap, and not just the furry or feathered variety. They're giving their time, their presence and their love (be it somewhat erratic and subject to a few juicy morsels). Kitty cuddles aside, the blessings don't stop there. Read on to discover why being a Cat Dad really is the cat's whiskers!

YOU'LL ALWAYS HAVE A PARTNER IN CRIME AND GRIME

Life with a Cat Dad is fun. Your laid-back attitude puts puss at ease and you're always up for an adventure. While some might flinch when their cat brings back a mousey gift, you simply shrug your shoulders and join in with a game of who's going to catch it first. Nothing fazes you, thanks to your cat.

The good news is you can really let yourself go with your fur buddy. While your cat has exacting standards, it's not about the way you look or yesterday's dirty dishes. Tatty makes for happy catty, so if you leave a mess or fail to look your very best – think unshaved and bristly, unkempt bed-head hair – your kitty really doesn't care. Stuff is where it's at for your cat; they love to stick their nose into something new, and as long as it's feline-friendly they'll be the cat that got the cream and you'll be daddy dream. So what if you leave a damp towel on the floor? It gives your kitty somewhere new to explore, and it's a cool hiding spot.

Human besties aside, nothing beats the relationship you have with your cat. Camaraderie feline-style is a step above the usual love and friendship in your life. You need each other, and not in a clingy, joined-at-the-hip way. This is man-to-cat appreciation, so effortless it's almost lackadaisical. 'Each to their own within the home' is your mantra. It keeps you calm and relaxed, and your cat super-chillaxed.

YOU HAVE YOUR OWN FELINE FITNESS COACH TO KEEP YOU IN SHAPE

Your puss prioritizes your health and fitness above everything else, and will give your routine a shake-up, should you need it. After all, as primary food-giver and all round mega Cat Dad, you need to be in tip-top condition to be at their beck and call. It's not simply about putting food in a dish, you need to be on the ball, quite literally, to keep them entertained.

Wellness is a two-way street, and your Moggie Motivator knows this. Early to rise is key to a positive attitude, hence your cat's 4 a.m. wake-up caterwaul. If that doesn't work, they'll go in for the kill with a claw to the toe or a carefully positioned butt in the face. Every feline knows that too much sleep makes a Cat Dad weak. Once up, they go into cat cajole mode, no megaphone required, just a hearty miaow and a nudge to the door with a deftly placed paw.

Once they have been fed, Kittie Keep Fit is next on the list. This is a tactical move by your puss to help you maintain focus throughout the day. Dogs might take their dads for a walk, but cats like to freestyle it. They understand the principles of a good workout: keep it fresh, keep it fun and keep your Cat Dad on the run. You might prefer your usual sprint al fresco, grabbing a coffee along the way, but your cat know that fitness starts in the home.

Toys are one way they keep you on your toes. Strategically placed and hard to spot, it's up to you to navigate a path by being quick on your feet. This is where your football tackling skills come in to play. Throw in a cat between the feet and you've a challenge to score, or at least reach the bathroom door without going offside. Make it in one piece and you'll be ready for a rest, but this is not the time to sit on the bench. Should they sneak in beside you, they'll give you the stare that says, 'Get that butt outta here!'

Who needs an expensive gym when your tabby can keep you trim anyway? This is about dedication and demonstration. Your welfare and their appreciation is where it's at, and that's what makes a cat a cat! And you are the luckiest (and fittest) Cat Dad in the world.

PAWSOME TIP

Kitty training can be fun for both of you. When playing games like 'feather on a stick', offer a treat as a reward, and give your cat some fuss. Encourage them to give you their paw in exchange for a treat or pick them up every time, as this will make it easier when you need to get hold of them for other things like giving them pills.

YOUR KITTY SLEEP BUDDY ENSURES YOU GET AS MUCH REST AS THEY THINK YOU NEED

Your cat knows that sleep is sacred. It is the holy grail of catdom and prized above all other pastimes. A juicy prawn might float their boat for a short while, but nothing beats the joy of a nap – and it's good for you too! There's nothing selfish about this. Choose the snooze and you'll never lose. But while cats can nod off at the drop of a hat, it might not be so easy for a stressed-out Cat Dad. With so much going on in your head, like when kitty should be fed and what delights to serve next, it's no wonder sleep eludes you. Never fear, your feline's here!

There's no better sleep guru than a cat. Just watching them in slumber is enough to make you dozy. Better still if they're curled up close. The rise and fall of their chest will put you in a hypnotic trance, and if that doesn't work they'll unleash their secret weapon – the power of the purr. You, dear Cat Dad, will be helpless in the face of it! This medicine for the soul is nothing short of a miracle cure, and it comes in the sweetest furry package.

Low, rumbling and super-soothing, it's a gentle melody that says, 'I love you; I am happy, all is well.' It's the mantra of choice for any moggie and a calming gift for you, because you're the greatest Cat Dad in the world. As wacky as it sounds, the purr falls at a level of hertz that is known to speed up recovery from all number of problems. From aching joints to broken bones and muscles torn or taut, a purr can have a healing effect on the human body. It also releases endorphins, and not just for your cat. You'll benefit from a sudden rush of feel-good hormones that works to lower blood pressure, ease stress and soothe migraines.

Let's face it, your cat is a healing wonder and the only sleep buddy you'll ever need! They may demand most of the mattress, leaving only a sliver for you to teeter on, but in return they put up with your bed-shaking snores. It's a compromise only a Cat Dad could make and it's worth taking, unless you want to stay awake to the tune of your moggie's miaows.

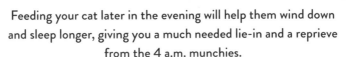

PAWSOME TIP

Feeding your cat later in the evening will help them wind down and sleep longer, giving you a much needed lie-in and a reprieve from the 4 a.m. munchies.

YOU'LL MAINTAIN A POSITIVE FEELGOOD ATTITUDE, THANKS TO A HEFTY DOSE OF CATTITUDE

Let's be honest, who doesn't want to be more cat? It might seem like their day is a repetitive cycle of eat, sleep, repeat, with a little play thrown in for good measure, but there's more to being feline fantastic than meets the eye. For a start, you need cattitude – that get-up-and-go, stick your nose into anything attitude. You don't know what's around the corner, but it could be a juicy burger from  next door's BBQ, or a butterfly to chase, so it's worth the effort. Optimism is key here, along with a can-do approach.

Cats are inquisitive, open-minded and ready to seize the moment, or the sausage, whichever comes first. They like to be in the midst of the action, or at least somewhere close by, so they can survey the outcome. Masters at the art of meditation and living in the moment, your moggie is a mindfulness guru, able to maintain a peaceful yet authoritative air.

Cats are great role models, and they lead by example. When you're feeling blue, they'll turn your frown upside down. When you need a break, they'll stretch out on your laptop to steal your attention and give screen time the big heave-ho. If you need to de-stress, they'll snuggle on to your chest, and should you need a pick-me-up, they're on hand with an impromptu paw-pummelling massage. They've also mastered more than one healing technique. You've heard of acupuncture, now get your claws into catipuncture! It's similar, but needle-free and delivered when you least expect it.

Your kitty not only does Zen, they **are** Zen, able to show you the secrets to a happy, peaceful and sometimes surprising existence. All you have to do is go with the feline feel-good flow.

PAWSOME TIP

Meditate with your moggie. Cats can pick up on peaceful vibes, and they might even take the opportunity to snuggle up next to you. If this happens, focus on the gentle sound of their breathing to promote stillness and generate feelings of calm for both of you.

'Of all God's creatures, there is only one that cannot be made slave of the leash. That one is the cat. If man could be crossed with the cat it would improve the man, but it would deteriorate the cat.'

MARK TWAIN

10 Reasons Why Being A Cat Dad Is Good For You

1

LOWERS ANXIETY AND STRESS

Petting your kitty releases feel-good chemicals in the brain, which in turn helps to relax the nervous system, meaning you're less likely to feel anxious or stressed.

2

IMPROVES GENERAL WELLBEING

Research suggests that owning a cat promotes psychological health. From cuddles to playtime, spending time together gives you a renewed sense of fulfilment.

3

DISPELS LONELINESS

Cats are great companions. They provide love and support and help you see the lighter side of life, so you're less likely to feel isolated or alone.

4

REDUCES RISK OF HEART DISEASE

Studies show that owning a cat helps to reduce stress levels, which has a direct effect on your cardiovascular health and can prevent heart attacks and strokes.

6 IMPROVES HEALING

Cats purr within a range of 10–110 Hz, which has a healing effect on the human body and has been known to speed up recovery from infections, broken bones and muscle injuries.

5 CAN PREVENT ALLERGIES

Children are less likely to develop a range of allergies when exposed to a cat at a young age. If you suffer with cat allergies, adopting a feline can help to build resistance.

8 HELPS WITH ONE-TO-ONE RELATIONSHIPS

Living with and loving a cat can improve your love life, by helping you to feel relaxed, more playful and open-hearted.

7 BOOSTS SELF-ESTEEM

Studies show that cat owners have higher levels of self-esteem. Researchers believe this is because they provide on-going social support to their humans.

10 SAVES YOUR LIFE

With their refined sense of smell and heightened hearing, cats pick on things that humans can't. They're alert to danger and can warn their owners of imminent threats.

9 SUPPORTS MENTAL HEALTH

Taking care of your cat gives you a sense of purpose and a reason to get up in the morning. Your cat needs and loves you, which has a positive effect on your mental wellbeing.

CHAPTER
6

Meet the Cat Dads

'Cats know how to obtain food without labour, shelter without confinement, and love without penalties.'

W.L. GEORGE

There are more Cat Dads than you might imagine. It is a growing trend, with more men jumping on the bandwagon faster than you can say 'sardine suppertime!' The joy that is all things cat is spreading throughout the world. The internet naturally has something to do with this phenomenon. The more we share, the more we are aware, and Cat Dads are making a stand. They're doing their bit for feline welfare, whether that's in adopting their own rescues or raising money and awareness for abandoned furries here and abroad.

Social media is buzzing with all things kitty and making a fuss of your puss is not just accepted, it's expected. No wonder then that Cat Dads are taking centre stage by putting their cats in the spotlight where they can be adored. From Twitter to TikTok, YouTube and more, it's about saying it loud and proud, being vocal about your passion for all things feline.

With this in mind, it's only right to introduce you to some of the Cat Dads making their mark, from social media favourites to fictional cat daddies who deserve a mention. These gentlemen are part of your inspirational tribe!

The Travelling Cat Dad

New York Lawyer, Dan Nguyen has become an internet sensation. This Cat Dad documents his travels alongside wife Olivia, and their three adorable felines: Sponge Cake, Mocha and Donut.

Find out more!
Instagram: @spongecake_thescottishfold
TikTok: @spongecake_cats

To start, can I ask a bit about your cats, their names/ages/ personality traits?
Sponge Cake (the ginger one) loves attention. When he is outside, he often comes up to people and asks for petting. Mocha (the cream one) lets people hug him and kiss him on the street. Donut (the white one) begs at the door to go outside every day. He loves it when people let him sniff them and pet him on the head. They're all two years old.

When did your love of all things feline begin?
I always loved animals. I had a dog growing up but always loved cats as well. We got our first cat a few years ago and became more and more attached! They are part of our family, and we love them so much.

What's the best thing about being a Cat Dad?
Cat cuddles! What I really like is the trust that they show me when I take them walking with me. They stay in my arms, or they sit on my backpack and explore their surroundings. It makes me feel proud that I can have that kind of relationship with them. Sponge Cake likes licking my face as well. I was not used to it in the beginning but now I appreciate his sentiment! I just love being around cats generally. It calms me down to pet them or let them rub themselves on my leg.

Are there any stand-out moments you could share about your cats?
Sponge Cake loves people and attention. We were once in the park when three ladies passed by and saw Sponge Cake walking on the grass. They were surprised and stopped to take a closer look. Sponge Cake walked over to the ladies and sat himself down so they could pet him! It was hilarious. From then on, I always called him a ladies' cat.

Once, Mocha and I were walking together in New York City. He was sitting on my backpack and, being ever curious, he placed his front paws on my shoulder and stood up to look around. This was already cute, but I wanted to encourage him further. So I held up my arms so that he could stand on them as well. He took the invitation and moved his front paws to my arms and his back paws to my shoulder. He stood up, sniffed, and kept on soaking in the experience. It was adorable and made me laugh.

Donut did one of the cutest things I have ever seen in my life. The sun had gone down and we were playing together in the park. We have fireflies in the summer in Central Park and they start lighting up during the evening. Donut ran around to chase them. Whenever he saw a light flare up, he jumped and tried to catch the fly.

What advice would you give newbie Cat Dads?
Pay attention to your cat's cues. Every cat is different and will respond to your actions. Try your best to understand what is making your cat satisfied, afraid and happy, and then adjust accordingly.

Finally, tell me a bit about your travels, and how it is travelling with your kitties?
My wife and I love travelling with our kitties. We couldn't imagine travelling without them now. They are real pros when it comes to flying. When we are at the airport, we open the top of their backpacks and they stick out their heads to explore the surroundings. They especially love it when we walk by the duty-free perfume shops so they can take in the smells. On the plane they sleep, groom themselves and basically relax during the

entire trip. And when they arrive at a new hotel room, they love to explore every nook and cranny of the room right away.

They particularly enjoyed travelling to Venice with us, taking in the smells of the canal waters. When we put them on the ground, they often walked right next to the canals and laid there to relax. Mocha particularly enjoys looking out on the water. He would probably stay there all day if we let him!

Famous Cat Dads

ERNST BLOFELD AND CAT (JAMES BOND)

Ernst Stavro Blofeld is one of the most infamous Bond villains, appearing in three of the novels (*Thunderball, On Her Majesty's Secret Service* and *You Only Live Twice*) and seven of the films. As a notorious arch-enemy of the super-suave 007, his character has been portrayed by many different actors, but one thing remains constant – his role as a Cat Dad. While his dubious morals and downright evil nature cannot be questioned, his ability to nurture his puss is an entirely different kettle of fish (and one where no sharks are required). Blofeld may be dastardly, but what he lacks in sweetness he more than makes up for when cuddling his kitty. The beautiful white Persian, who remains nameless in the books and films, is the centre of his world and always at the forefront of the shot, a clever ploy by the filmmakers who must have realized the lure of the feline. While Bond parades a bevy of beauties on his arm, Blofeld has only one love – his cat – which begs the question, 'Who is the real villain of the piece?'

JAMES BOWEN AND BOB

Street cat Bob and his doting dad James Bowen had a unique relationship, which began in 2007 when James stumbled upon the injured and abandoned ginger cat near his home. James, who had been homeless for many years previously, was dealing with drug addiction, but decided to take Bob in and care for him. These two lost souls found each other and formed an unbreakable bond, which James wrote about in the multinational bestselling book *A Street Cat Named Bob*. The book was turned into a successful film, with Bob in the starring role. Known for his knitted scarves and friendly manner, Bob and owner James were a common sight on the streets of London, busking and entertaining passersby with their endearing relationship.

JON ARBUCKLE AND GARFIELD

Lovable, leary and super-hairy, that's Garfield, the wise-cracking ginger cat with the big attitude and an even bigger appetite for lasagne, first published as a comic strip under the same name in 1978. This Cat Dad to kitty duo is the brainchild of Jim Davis, who created the comic to chronicle the humorous ups and downs of their daily life. While Jon is long-suffering and often outsmarted by his clever feline, he is without a doubt a doting Cat Dad. He puts up with Garfield's antics and laziness, because at the end of the day life would be dull without him. From delivering whiffy cat burps to swiping the dinner from his plate, Garfield may test his love, but one thing Jon is firm about is his love for his cat.

'You will always be lucky if you know how to make friends with strange cats.'

OLD AMERICAN
PROVERB

Conclusion

Cats are a conundrum. From crazy and complicated to cute and cuddly, they're impossible to pin down – and you wouldn't really want to, would you? After all, you're a Cat Dad, and that makes you just as much of a mystery (especially among other males who secretly admire your cool cat ways). Like those of the feline variety, you do your own thing, which makes you the perfect pairing. The bond you share with your kitty is fur-to-skin deep and something worth celebrating. We've already mentioned all the ways in which you're truly awesome, but the last word should really go to your cat. So here it is...

Cat Dad, You're Meow-vellous!

Further Reading

Sophie Collins, *How to Raise a Happy Cat (So They Love You More Than Anyone Else)*, Ivy Press (2023)

Catherine Davidson, *Why Does My Cat Do That? Answers to the 50 Questions Cat Lovers Ask*, Ivy Press (2014)

Alison Davies, *The Cat Purrsonality Test*, White Lion Publishing (2021)

Jackson Galaxy, Cat Daddy: *What the World's Most Incorrigible Cat Taught Me About Life, Love, and Coming Clean*, TarcherPerigee (2013)

Dr Yuki Hattori, *What Cats Want: An Illustrated Guide for Truly Understanding Your Cat*, Bloomsbury Publishing (2020)

Carol Kaufman, *97 Ways to Make a Cat Like You*, Workman (2015)

Pippa Mattinson and Lucy Easton, *The Happy Cat Handbook*, Ebury Press (2019)

Amy Shojai, *Cat Life: Celebrating the History, Culture & Love of the Cat*, Furry Muse Publications (2019)

cats.org.uk/help-and-advice
The one-stop shop from Cats Protection, which provides advice on all aspects of owning and caring for your cat.

icatcare.org
The ultimate resource for cat care with an A–Z guide on health conditions.

thecatgallery.co.uk
Quality gifts for cats, and those who love them.

thecatsite.com
A comprehensive site, with forums on cat behaviour, health problems and living with your cat.

yourcat.co.uk
The website of the popular magazine, which has interesting features on cat behaviour, training your cat and top tips on cat care.

About the Author

Alison Davies has over 20 years' experience of living with numerous cats and has been writing about them for many years too. She writes for a wide selection of magazines and has penned books on a variety of topics including animals, astrology and self-help. Her cat credentials include the books *Be More Cat, Cat Purrsonality Test, Dog Pawsonality Test* and *Cattitude Journal*, as well as writing for *Take a Break Pets*.

About the Illustrator

Marie Åhfeldt is a freelance illustrator based in Stockholm, Sweden, who specialises in editorial illustration, animal drawings and artwork for children.

Quarto

First published in 2023 by White Lion Publishing,
an imprint of Quarto.
1 Triptych Place
London, SE1 9SH

www.Quarto.com

A catalogue record for this book is available from the British Library.

ISBN 978 0 7112 8515 6
Ebook ISBN 978 0 7112 8516 3

10 9 8 7 6 5 4 3 2 1

Publisher: Jessica Axe
Commissioning Editor: Andrew Roff
Editor: Bella Skertchly
Designer: Francesca Corsini

Printed in China